ERIK KESSELS

COMPLETE
AMATEUR

Corraini Edizioni

START THIS BOOK

START IT WHEREVER YOU LIKE. FRONT TO BACK. BACK TO FRONT. EITHER WAY, EVERY DOUBLE PAGE HAS QUOTES, SHORT READS, VISUAL EXAMPLES AND MOTIVATIONS, ALL DESIGNED TO WORK OUT YOUR AMATEUR MUSCLE. NO STRUCTURE. NO ORDER.

PRE

Most careers are built on a foundation of similar bricks: education, accumulated knowledge, experience, professional know-how, technical skills, efficiency, ability to perform under pressure, and publicly recognized successes. The very things defining most professional careers are exactly what causes creativity (and careers) to stagnate.
It doesn't matter what industry you're in, if you think you know it all and you have nothing left to learn, you've basically given up on developing your professional abilities. Once you reach this point, the reality is that your best work is probably behind you, at least for now. Creative freedom is restricted by preconceived ideas of professional creativity. Typical markers of success become creative anchors. They stop you from taking risks because you can't afford to get it wrong. They stop you from trying new things because new is unpredictable. Amateurs are free of the traps of professionalism because if you don't know the rules, the rules don't matter. The amateurs' lack of technical skills prevents them from seeing the most obvious creative solution, which makes experimentation their only option.

FACE

Amateurs aren't held back by skills they don't have. It's the way amateurs embrace improvisation that makes their work so exciting, and that's why professionals should embrace it more often. But don't go thinking that amateurism is new. It's not. Throughout history, amateurs have been applying their naivety and innovation to things they know nothing about, with notable successes. A devout monk fathered modern genetics in his spare time. A nanny photographed New Yorkers better than professionals. A blind lawyer opted for opera and sold out theatres. This book celebrates amateurism. It's not just a source of amateur inspiration, it's a guide to letting go of everything you know and embracing things you know nothing about. Knowing less can be good for you, and particularly good for your career. What you know is holding you back. What if knowing nothing is the key to learning more? As an 87-year-old Michelangelo once said, "I'm still learning." (Actually, this quote is misattributed – likely by an amateur – but it's comforting to think the Italian master thinks as we do.)

THE BEST WAY TO OBSERVE A FISH

IS TO BECOME A FISH.

JACQUES COUSTEAU

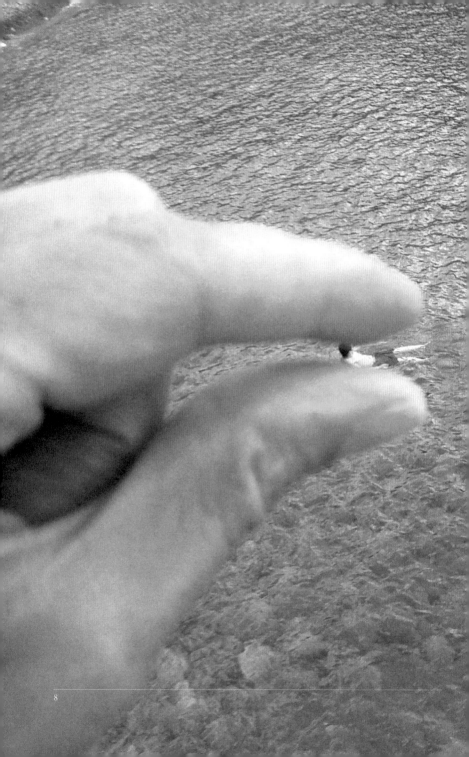

BEHAVE
LIKE AN
OUTSIDER.

WHAT MADE

PICK UP THIS BOOK?

Nobody told you to.
You didn't have to.
No.
You went with your gut.
Something you used to do.
Before you knew the rules.
But you went with your gut just now and that says
something.
It's the first sign that you're ready to lose control.
Break the rules.
Don't expect to get control of this book.
You can't. You shouldn't.
That's the whole point.
This book ~~wants you to~~
needs you to lose control.
And don't think you can avoid it.
This book has no structure.
Go ahead. Start it wherever you want.
However you feel. Front to back. Back to front.
Every double page is different so you won't run into
a problem. Only solutions.
They come in quotes, short reads, visual examples
and motivations.
You picked up this book based on your gut.
But "gut" is such an ugly word.
How about "amateur"?
You know that instinct that's brought you to this point.
This book will ~~help you to~~
force you to rediscover your inner amateur.

Coming up with ideas for furniture designs is always within your reach. Product designers understand that packaging is often just as important as its product. Here the packaging forms a completely new product, an unforeseen design gem. The box as backrest and seat, with the pizza as a soft cushion on top. Make yourself comfortable!

MAKE YOURSELF COMFORTABLE

THE IMPORTANCE OF

Being alone is important for the creative process, but there are two more necessary components: time and environment. There is no better encapsulation of all three than the homely shed. A place where you retreat to. Famously only placed in the backyard, a shed is where things are made, but never presented. A shed is where you make mistakes in the dark. A shed is somewhere you disappear to. Roald Dahl exclusively wrote in his shed, which is now a monument to his life. Arthur Miller built a shed and used the time to conjure up *Death of a Salesman*. By the time the shed was finished, he used it to write the play. You don't have to own a shed to isolate, but you have to come up with your own version of a shed. Close the door. No one can see you. No one can disturb you. Not even yourself. Essentially, a place to be fiddling where no one is looking. A walk in the park where you get lost and suddenly pick up a strange conversation. Maybe you find something lying on the ground that doesn't fit. Fiddling doesn't have to be physical. It can be all mental. For instance, good ideas sometimes spark when you are on the toilet and in the shower. It's because your brain is blocked from things happening outside. You're cut off. Want great ideas? Try going to the toilet without your phone.

ISOLATION

Your mind will wander in ways you had forgotten, as it used to do before we were constantly communicating. With the constant barrage of ideas from apps and professional trade websites, you're only exposed to what's already been done. It's a poison to creativity. Sure, there are great references, but it's not a starting point to find new inspiration. The important thing is that these metaphorical sheds, like the real ones, are limited to a small scope and size. You can't build a ship in a shed. You can't go to a shed to make a house. Perhaps the most restrictive isolation is on an airplane. You cannot move. Your phone is switched off. You're limited to a certain amount of activities. It's almost as if the higher you are up off the ground, the less gravity your ideas have and suddenly they float up into your line of sight. Isolation sometimes works in groups, but the group still needs to be isolated. That's why most research centres are out of the way. It's because they are designed to get the group members dependent on each other. Designed to not be distracting. You live, eat, sleep and breathe with the same isolated group, off the grid, and suddenly there is stimulus. Like a group of people trapped on a desert island, you are forced to come up with ideas.

"Don't play with your food," is something we're told from an early age. The designer Duc Nguyen chucked this rule out the window and these beautifully erotic images were the result.

Ria van Dijk is a Dutch woman whose life is seen from the point of view of a fairground shooting gallery. The chronological series begins in 1936, when a 16-year-old girl from Holland picks up a gun and shoots at the target in a shooting gallery. Every time she hits the target, it triggers the

shutter of a camera and a portrait of the girl in firing pose is taken and given as a prize. And so, a lifelong love affair with the shooting gallery begins. This series documents almost every year of her life: a woman's biography from an unusual perspective.

If you don't know what you're doing, you're often at your best. Thinking without thinking. You are born with the ability to be an amateur. But you have to turn pro. Amateur is primal.

These boards to stick your head through can be found in touristic destinations and are often very predictable… But why not make your own at home and have fun with it?

I AM NOT REALLY CERTAIN HOW ORIGINAL MY CONTRIBUTION

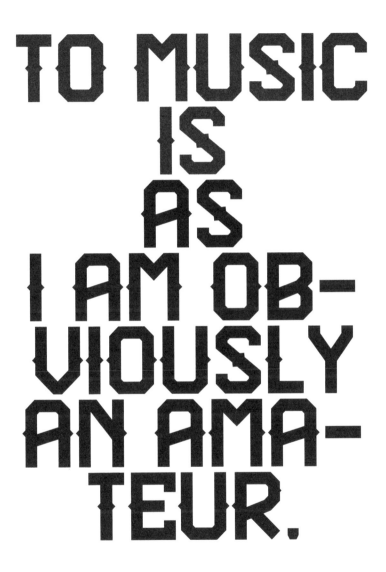

TO MUSIC IS AS I AM OBVIOUSLY AN AMATEUR.

PATTI SMITH

Doing something the right way doesn't mean it's the only way. And even though doing something wrong may not be right, it could be better. Like Levi Strauss, who made pants out of denim back when that was as foreign as wearing socks on your ears. While mastering a skill requires a complete understanding of everything, it also relies on your ability to question everything. Like a kid in school, you should always have your hand up. Even if you know the answer. This is the amateurs' advantage. They are constantly curious and eagerly experimenting. They don't know the right way and that's why they have a higher chance of doing it better (keep in mind this has no statistical basis, but is more of an amateur analysis). Blind trust is an element of amateurism that is crucial to the craft. A trust in yourself – that you don't recognize in the moment – that allows you to act without doubt, misstep, or caution. Like a painter who attacks a canvas versus a master who stands back scratching their chin, imagining six ways to Sunday. Going in blind is sometimes the only way to see clear. Let's take the sport of rowing as an example. A highly technical sport that consumes its athletes and demands 25/8 of their time. Your average rower is typically tall, lanky, and academic – even a bit nerdy. Maybe it's the mathematical precision of the technique that attracts such high-minded individuals. Unlike sports like basketball, where bad math ends with losing a free throw, bad math in rowing could literally send you out of the boat. If the oar hits a snag in the wave – a crab – the power of everything leading up to it launches you into ice-cold water, which could result in hypothermia if not treated immediately. It is believed the rower's first-ever stroke is and always will be their most perfect. It's because you're not thinking. You're just reacting. Everything after is simply an attempt to replicate that perfect stroke. But not just replicate it once. The goal is to make it happen every time. All your training is an effort to replicate that first stroke. In essence, become pro at being amateur. Also known as "making it look easy." The "thoughtless stroke" of the novice rower is purely instinctual and natural. No coaching or inner voice of self-doubt. This thoughtless stroke is referred to in the rowing community with positivity; like an unattainable goal that every rower strives for. In a way, it's the positive equivalent of saying "beginner's luck." Soon enough, rowers start to love the idea of chasing the thoughtless stroke. This relates to the Latin root of the word amateur, *amare*:

TO LOVE

Artist Daniel Eatock re-appropriated this idea from his mother. Maybe it started as an accident or out of laziness. Either way, it wasn't deliberate but the action of an amateur

that created a habit, turning an ordinary bowl into an extraordinary art object. It's a stunning example of amateur inspiration.

Sometimes creativity is your only option. In the 50s
and 60s, foreign music was banned in the Soviet Union.
People didn't want to miss out on the likes of Elvis Presley,

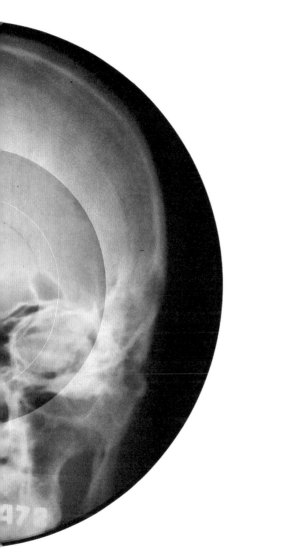

The Beatles, and The Rolling Stones, so they came up with some pretty ingenious ways of smuggling the music into the country; like printing records on x-rays.

DO IT LIKE YOU DON'T KNOW

ERIK KESSELS

WHAT YOU'RE DOING

THE BEST
RECIPES FOR
CREATIVITY...

... ARE NOT
ON THE
MENU.

"I SET MYSELF CHALLENGES EVERY TIME
I WORK. IDEALLY, I APPROACH EVERYTHING
AS THOUGH IT'S THE FIRST TIME
– WITH A BEGINNER'S MIND AND
AN AMATEUR'S LOVE."

WILLEM DAFOE

Sam Barsky threw caution to the wind and took up freestyle knitting as a way to memorialize all of the places he's been. Thankfully, he's better with a pair of knitting needles than he is with a camera, but it's the combination that makes

this project a warm, fuzzy winner. In case you were wondering, his wife Deborah does not share his love of knitting, although apparently, he has tried to convert her.

Stop reading this book and try boredom! Stare at bathroom tiles until you see the face of Jesus. Read the Terms and Agreements of your favourite app. Stand in a long line. Call a hotline and get put on hold. Boring, huh? That's ok. That's the point. You were forced to be alone with your thoughts for a moment. Those first few moments are agonizing. All you can think about is what you're gonna do immediately after, but the reality is that this is necessary to be an amateur. An amateur has the time to be bored.

STOP READING THIS BOOK

A woman loves her husband so much she wishes to never see him with anyone else but her, not even in pictures. Rather than throw them out entirely, she makes them her

own. Her selfish love for him is more important than the pictures themselves. Like a dog pissing on a tree, her markings on the pictures let everyone know, "He's mine."

HELMUT SMITS - *RAINBOW*

Who knew the end of a rainbow could be found on your
windshield. Helmut Smits' *Rainbow* has a childlike curiosity to it. Putting paint on the windshield sounds like something you'd get in trouble for. The best ideas seem to work
like that. The result is a permanent rainbow, or at least until
it rains. Six little dabs of paint transform an everyday car
into a rainbow chaser, turning every vista into one of colour,
happiness and magic.

TRANS-FORM YOURSELF INTO THE AMATEUR

Go back to the time before you became a professional, stripping yourself entirely of the rules and expectations that come with it. Go back to the time before school. Before you were taught how to colour in the lines. Go back to the time when you were totally primitive. Wipe the slate clean, dust off the professional baggage, and revert to tabula rasa. Metaphorically speaking, isolate yourself. Now it's important to remember that you don't have to constantly be an amateur, but a method like this manifests certain ideas. You realize things that you don't notice with professional blinders on. Sometimes you have to behave childish or stupid to revert to an amateur way of thinking and doing. Don't let that scare you. Remember, when you didn't know how to do it, you weren't afraid of making mistakes. After struggling to develop as a traditional painter, Jackson Pollock reverted to a method of painting attributed to most toddlers, who mindlessly drip paint on a canvas.

The stars of a creative dog
grooming competition,
the wackiest-looking pets
are exhibited in shows
full of amateur surprises.

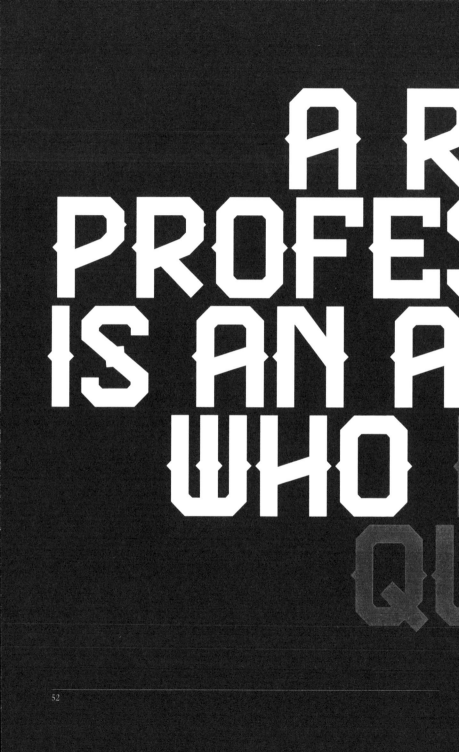

A R
PROFES
IS AN A
WHO
QU

Break up with yourself. Too often we are confined by what we think we know and are good at. We act like we know what we like, don't like, etc. So, look at yourself in the mirror, or even write yourself a letter, letting yourself know it's over. Meet someone new inside of yourself. Chances are you'll meet someone you never could've imagined. Fall in love again.

BREAK UP WITH YOURSELF

GREEN SMILEY

Canvases don't always come bound and stretched into white squares. Dutch artist Bart Eysink Smeets uses nature as a canvas with his *Smiley Tree Triptych*. With nothing more than a green thumb and a ladder, Bart transforms his surroundings to reflect how he feels. His uncomplicated approach, and simplistic smiley face, allow the work to speak for itself. Look around you. Look where no one's looking. There may be a canvas waiting to express how you feel.

PUT YOUR NOS
AND HAVE

HIS SENTENCE
T DREAM.

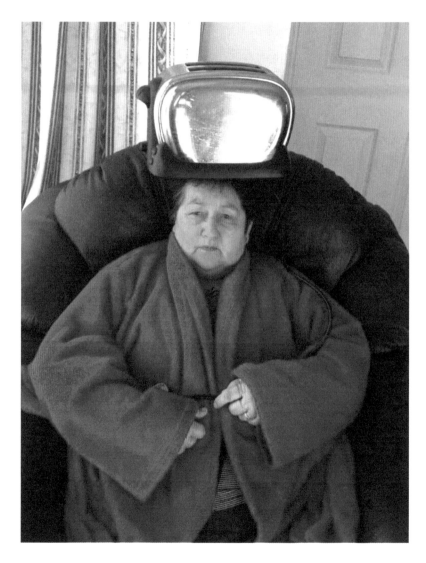

QUICK. OFF THE TOP OF YOUR HEAD...
...WHAT ARE SOME WAYS TO SELL JUNK?

THIS LADY OF THE HOUSE
HAS A COUPLE SUGGESTIONS.

The photographer of these postcards from the 60s was

clearly driving a red car, which he never left out of sight.

Amateur used to be positive. Where did the meaning get lost? As far as modern lingo goes, "amateur" is used to describe one's lack of skill. Could it be that the competitive nature of activity has skewed our ability to perceive any joy from what we do? Do we forget that the reason why we do what we love comes simply from the act of loving it? Consider this: The tendency to overthink comes from self-doubt, insecurity, or the desire to please. Oftentimes overthinking leads to not doing. An amateur does not overthink because they don't know the stakes. The rules don't apply because they don't know the consequences.

AMATEUR USED TO BE POSITIVE

Before Instagram, passionate and amateur photographers expressed their talents in camera clubs. The beauty of these photographs is often only discovered years after they've been made. Ralph Smith (Derby, England) is such a photographer. He produced many images between 1985 and 1999 and won several international competitions at the time. He was an active member of these camera clubs and his last was the Rolls Royce camera club in Derby. Now, years later, his work is considered slightly exotic and from a period when photographs had to tell a story. Instead of showing snippets and suggestions of stories, Smith's staged work is at times extremely literal in its interpretation. A very nice example of this is the photograph he titled *Window Shopping*, of a window frame holding two shopping bags. His works, especially when shown in a different context such as these pages, become disturbingly weird, artistic, and even sometimes surrealistic.

SURREALISM
BY RALPH SMITH

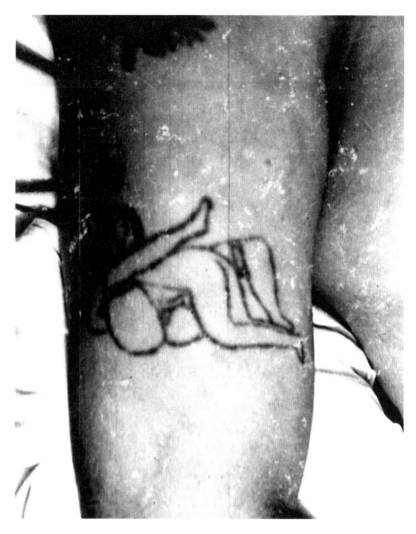

Tattoos on deceased Cuban prostitutes show how drawings were used as a menu of positions for customers, due to occasional language barriers.

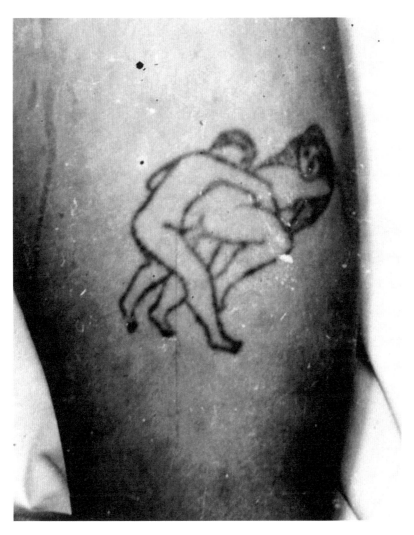

As François Rabelais, the French humorist and monk (who never got laid), astutely said, "The appetite grows with eating."

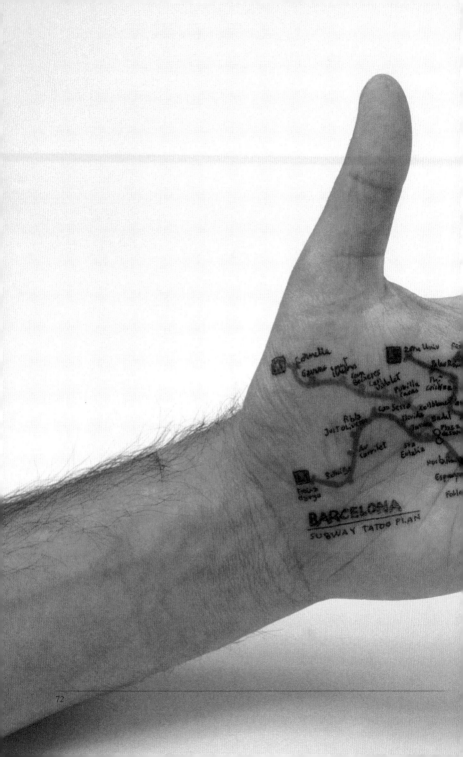

Wouldn't it be incredibly nice to always have a metro map handy when you need it? This extremely useful tattoo was made by the Catalan designer Martí Guixé. He designed a series of handy tattoos, including an image of a coin that beggars can have tattooed in their palms. For a different tattoo, Guixé changed an index finger into a ruler by placing measurements on the side of the finger.

Artist and designer Helmut Smits has built his own private
Nascar out of shopping bags, garbage bags, plastic foil,
tape, and air. It shows what you can do by having a great

idea, recycling plastic, and a lot of determination. On an additional positive note, this car has a 100% clean air emission. (Even though you can't actually drive it.)

Outsider artist Dalton Ghetti takes miniature sculptures to the extreme with his pencil carving.

Jens Sundheim is a German man fascinated with webcams and security cameras. He has an uncontrollable need to collect their locations online, and he also travels around the world to visit them! His wife, at home, sits at a computer and waits for his call. As soon as Jens encounters

the camera, she records him online by taking a screenshot.
Not only does Jens have an impressive amount of self-por-
traits, but he's also travelled the world! Don't expect to see
any exhibitions unless there's a webcam nearby.

Finally, printing images no longer has to be a mechanical procedure. At www.thehumanprinter.org, a whole team of people is ready to handprint any image you want. Correction: to dot for you with coloured markers. The team members are more often described as "slow" and "tired quickly" than "precise" or "reliable," but it is a painstaking job. The Human Printer is the ultimate example of our natural response to the great convenience that machines offer us today. It shows once again that there is a growing need to make things by hand again and thus give them personality. You have to love grid dots to get started with this collective.

I AM ALWAYS DOING WHAT I CANNOT DO YET,

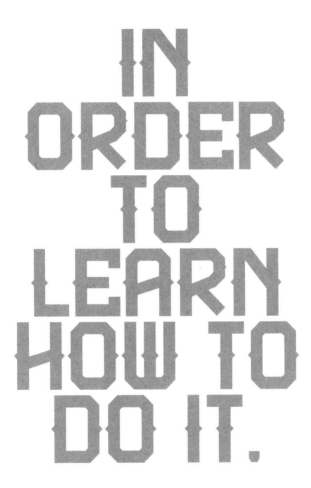

IN ORDER TO LEARN HOW TO DO IT.

VINCENT VAN GOGH

A toilet is a place for reflection. While dedicating your attention to a single task, your mind is free to wander. Oh what ideas come from the throne of thought! Moreover, what better place to hold a talk. To flush out ideas.

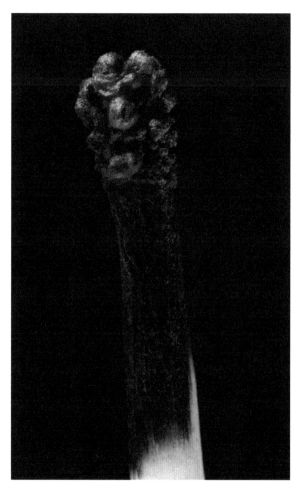

This creepy cabinet of wonder was created b
beek, a graphic designer from Amsterdam. A
these appear to be a series of creepy sculptur
closer inspection they reveal burnt matches.
any burnt match. No, certainly not! Verbeek

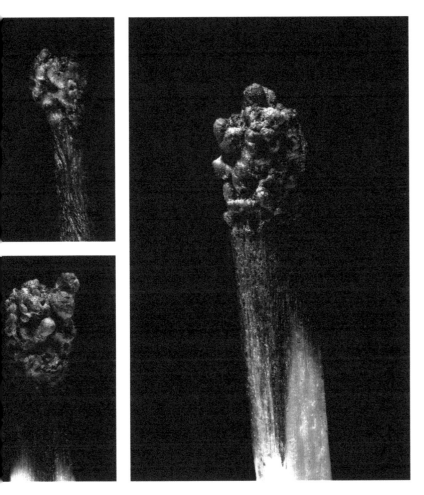

of matches to make a good selection. The result is amazing and monumental, especially if you imagine how many evenings Verbeek spent with his magnifying glass looking at used matches. Finally, a tip: know what you're getting yourself into if you light another candle.

MAKE ART THAT
LOOKS GOOD
ABOVE PEOPLE'S
COUCHES.

Back in my day, we didn't have smartphones.

We didn't have cameras watching us.

We didn't constantly text.

We didn't take photos to show what we ate for lunch.

No, back in my day, we used what we had.

For example, when your grandfather and I started dating,

I knew he had a reputation for being a bit of a Casanova.

Not just with me, but with many people at one time.

Before deciding if he was the one to spend the rest of my life

with, I needed to ensure he was on his best behaviour.

I'm not a detective by trade, but I like to think of myself as

an amateur sleuth.

Back in my day, there weren't fancy computer jobs,

but simple jobs you did with your hands.

Your grandfather was a painter who rode his bicycle to work.

One morning, I poked a hole in one of his paint canisters

and followed him.

I was surprised by two things: One, was how he rode to

work. It was never in a straight line, but rather in twists

and turns that suggested a playful man.

A person who enjoyed the music of life.

Two, was that he was fucking my best friend.

Spanish photographer David de la Cruz analyses how restaurateurs promote their food to passers-by. They often use a three-dimensional image of what is served inside. We are all familiar with the enlarged ice cream cone and the giant French fries bag in front of an ice cream parlour or snack bar, but in the centre of the Italian city of Palermo, this phenomenon reaches unprecedented new heights. What about a gigantic chicken cut from Styrofoam, impaled on the base of a postcard rack? In any case, when I saw it, I gasped! All the food came out of my mouth with laughter.

FOOD
PROMOTION

There are two houses that are special to me, both which
I noticed in recent years: one in the Netherlands and one
in Singapore. On the house in a Dutch cemetery, the windows and door are impossible to open. It is closed forever
even though there is a special step leading up to the door.
Symbolic, perhaps. Or totally unintentional. It is a striking,
detonating stone among messy tombstones with the house

number 34 on it, why 34? It looks a bit strange to have a numbered tombstone in a graveyard.

This house in Singapore decorated with air conditioners is just as curious. Its inhabitants must be better protected from the heat than anyone else. I want to stop at both houses. In both cases, extreme ugliness is transformed into extreme amateur beauty.

No matter how hard Arnold flexes his muscles in this mural, you don't need an eye tracking device to know where everyone's eyes will be drawn. Whether the window was there first or the painting, we'll never know, but it's just waiting for someone to stick their head out the window to enjoy the view.

EYE
TRACKING

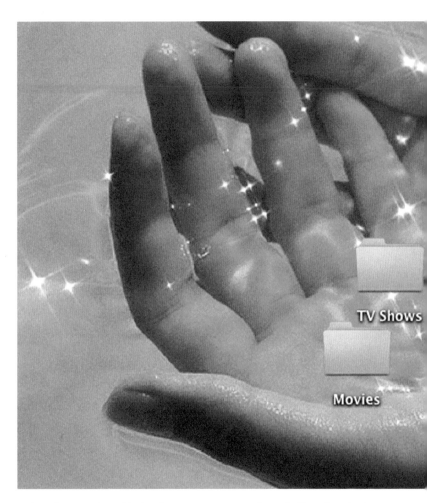

Thank you for all the images we receive daily. Copied, re-cycled, or mixed. Because of this abundance, it sometimes seems as if everything has already been done. Yet every once in a while a surprising gem floats to the top. Like this fairy-tale way to decorate your desktop. Two glittering soft

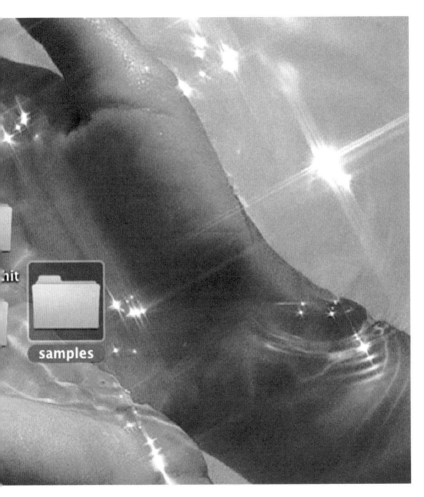

hands gently scoop a few folders up. As if they are small
fish that could slip away at any moment. The person responsible has probably already been forgotten due to the
endless copying of the beautiful image. Thank you to the
anonymous creator.

Rop van Mierlo is a graphic designer and fond of animals.
At least, if you are to believe his book *Wild Animals*.
With the so-called "wet in wet" technique, he illustrated
countless wild animals in an almost uncontrollable way.
Van Mierlo puts the wet ink on paper and lets it drift with

great feeling in any direction that he wants. It produces amazing results. This is how an elephant runs at a happy trot across the page and you can see the beautiful fur of a tiger captured here. All it took to tame this beast was a sheet of paper, two colours, and a little water.

Adolf Hitler was a painter.
Joseph Stalin was a pool shark.
Charles Manson was a musician.
Osama Bin Laden was a martial artist.
Nero was a singer.
Kim Jong-il was a film enthusiast.
If only these men hadn't given up on their original passions.
Maybe they needed a little encouragement.
Either way, the world would've been a far better place had
they not chosen their "careers" in evil.

The Italian Daniele Pario Perra shows us images of special objects and sculptures that he discovered during his travels through Europe. He displays works by amateurs who appear to have created designs often in imaginative ways. For example, a bench made of skateboards. A clothespin of two chop-

sticks. Or even the diving mask to cut onions without crying! Here is a work of art by a seller of cuddly toys. He turned his means of transport inside out and thus turned his van into a shop window. The result is a real attraction. I'm wondering what it would look like if he drove the car like this?

"I EQUATE FILMS WITH SANDCASTLES. YOU
GET A BUNCH OF MATES AND YOU GO DOWN
AND YOU SAY I'M GOING TO BUILD THIS
GREAT SANDCASTLE AND YOU BUILD IT.
THEN, THE TIDE COMES IN AND IN TWENTY
MINUTES IT'S JUST SMOOTH SAND. AND THAT
STRUCTURE YOU MADE IS IN EVERYBODY'S
MEMORY AND THAT'S IT."

ROBERT ALTMAN

HAMBURGER

THOMAS MAILAENDER

MAKING MASKS

Paul Bogaers is inspired by traditional African masks and combines this with recycled objects to create his own take on tradition, culture and reappropriation. It's amazing how a couple of tweaks to an existing object turn it into an entirely new creature.

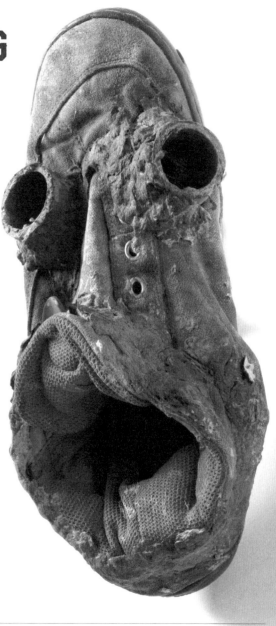

Go for a walk without headphones. Not to mention the ear wax and bacterial infections they cause, headphones block out the outside world. Maybe a passing line from a stranger could be the key to your whole voice as an artist. Maybe you need to hear the sounds of nothing. Of wind. Of birds hitting windows. Maybe that's what will kick-start you into actually doing something.

Be extremely busy. This is a complete contradiction to everything above, but sometimes boredom takes many forms. Boredom can be found in a busy schedule. Some of the best work comes when you're in a rush. The activities don't even have to be related to your end goal, but the constant task-oriented motives will keep your brain stimulated. When an idea truly does fall from the sky, you'll feel it. You won't expect it, because you're too focused on the tasks.

"WHAT'S VERY FUNNY IS WHEN YOU SEE
AMATEURS FILMING SOMETHING,
THEY DO SOME THINGS NO PROFESSIONALS
WOULD DARE TO DO.
THEY INSTINCTIVELY DO THINGS THAT ARE
VERY AVANT-GARDE AND USEFUL."

WILLIAM KLEIN

Bas Kosters is a Dutch fashion designer with a unique, colourful style directly inspired by amateur knitting and quilting patterns. The influence of amateurs is very apparent.

It gives his work a playful, almost childish quality which is offset by his edgy, contemporary take on traditional garments.

Fill your calendar brick-tight.

Even if you've got nothing to do.

Find something.

Make many many hours.

Harken back to the time when you were bussing tables and doing school and working a second job and managing a relationship and trying to write that novel.

When time was more valuable than money.

When you only had 10 minutes of 24 hours to work on what you loved.

For as rich as a professional can get, they will never get the value of those 10 minutes.

They've got all the time in the world.

People doing things for them to make their day less busy.

It takes them 10 hours to do what you did in 10 minutes.

Because you had no choice.

You were too busy.

If you siphon off your creativity, sometimes you're forced to realize what your best ideas are.

GET
BUSY
BUSY
BUSY
BUSY
BUSY
BUSY
BUSY

THE STONE THAT WENT BACK HOME

Experts rely on tools, know-how, and exposure. Amateurs are sometimes only armed with ideas, and Dutch artist Bart Eysink Smeets had a small idea with big results. He learned that Netherlands' famous boulders had travelled from other countries via glaciers during the Ice Age. Like an extreme version of a kid kicking a rock all the way home, Bart transported one of these 200,000-year-old boulders to its rightful Scandinavian home. Bart's not a geologist, a scientist, urban planner or archaeologist. He is just an amateur who simply wanted to "kick a rock home" because that's where it belonged.

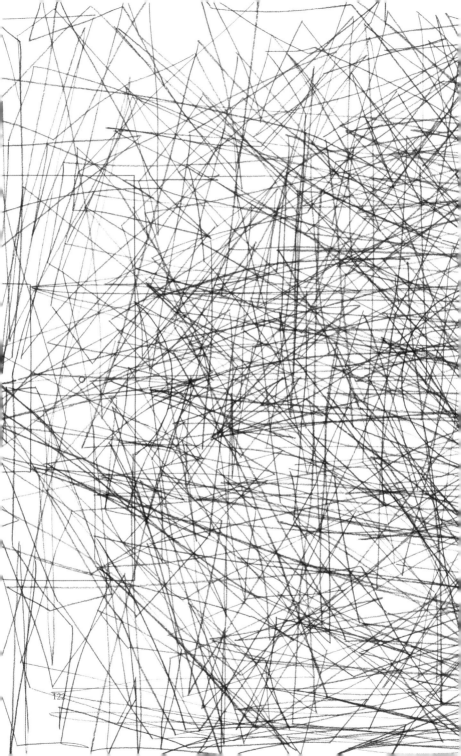

At first I thought of a doodle of a three-year-old child.
Or perhaps a failed Spirograph drawing? But if you look
closely you can recognize the lines of a football field through
the scratches. For a while Joachim Schmid from Berlin
made these drawings while watching a football match.
From kick-off, until the final whistle, Schmid followed
the movements of the game with his pencil. Here you see
Hertha BSC against Aberdeen, sometime in 2002.
Complete with throw-ins, corners and of course the goals.
Only when the game was stopped did his pencil have a rest.
This one game ended in 1-0 for the Germans.

Inspiration is there for the taking. Sometimes in the form of a rolled-up Marilyn Monroe poster held flat by four trophies. The flea market seller of this poster could not have come up with a more striking presentation.
Originality often arises from an accidental combination of elements that have little or nothing to do with each other. So keep looking around.

ACCIDENTAL COMBINATION

Chances are you've never heard of Michael Faraday. Don't worry, you're not the only one. He was a bookbinder's apprentice with almost no formal schooling who went on to become one of the most influential scientists of all time, and it all happened because he got bored at work. Faraday was born in 1791 as the third of four children. The family was too poor to send their children to school and at fourteen years of age, Faraday became an apprentice bookbinder. Surrounded by books all day, everyday, curiosity quickly got the better of him and he became an avid reader. Most of the books he had access to were scientific literature, which nurtured his keen interest in all things science, electricity in particular. After seven years binding (and reading) countless books, he quit his job to pursue his interest in chemistry. Without the appropriate social status, and no

HISTORI-
CAL

formal education to speak of, the science world did not exactly welcome him with open arms. But there were a couple of open-minded gentlemen who saw his potential. Faraday took his chance and ran with it. He went on to invent the Bunsen burner (yes, that thing you burnt your fingers on in high school), he discovered benzene and essentially created the first electric motor and electric generator. His work greatly contributed to the fields of electromagnetism and electrochemistry, and he was largely responsible for developing practical applications for electricity, particularly in terms of technology. As a deeply religious man, he believed fame and fortune were unbecoming of a Christian. He turned down both the offer of a knighthood and the offer to be buried in Westminster Abbey. But they eventually stuck him in there anyway, with a memorial plaque next to Isaac Newton.

AMATEUR

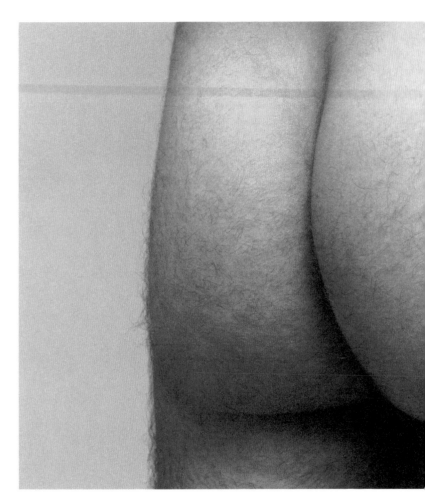

In times of overall terror, it's often best to have some fun in your back pocket (or maybe closer to the skin). French artist and photographer Thomas Mailaender must have had this idea, because he tattooed the word "FUN" in unmistakable block letters and on a rather unusual place: his right buttock.

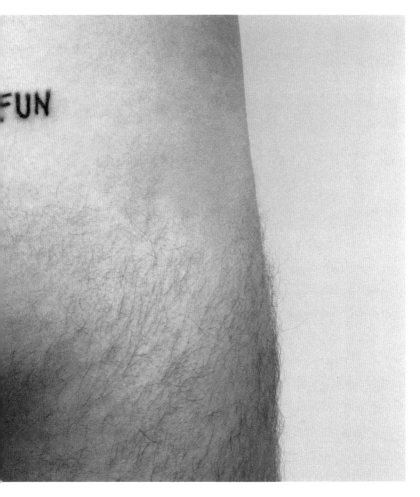

FUN

How much clearer can you get! Such a tattoo seems to be made for private connections, but his taking a picture of it suggests he wants to inspire others! Perhaps Thomas has conveyed his feeling a bit too literally in people's eyes, but it certainly left an indelible impression on me.

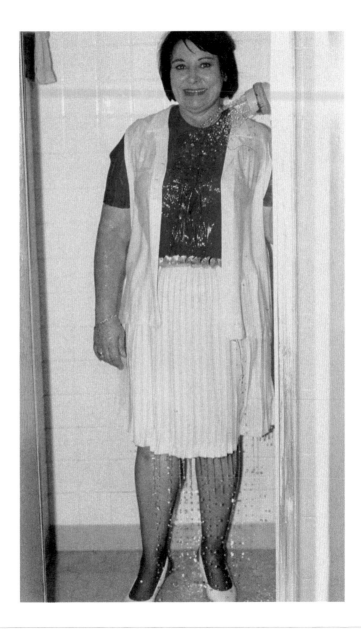

ACTIVE IDEAS:

Disappear, but leave a note.

Take a shower, but keep it cold.

Turn off your phone, but play music.

Take away a tool,
but make sure it's the one you use the most.

Try to come up with six band names in a world where
virtually every word and common phrase is already taken.

Write yourself a brief.
Try to do it in 5 minutes.
Try to do the worst version of it.

Sit on a toilet with your pants on.
Use it as a chair. A throne of ideas.
Flush so people listening don't get worried.

Mingering Mike (not his real name) not only followed through, but he created an illustrious (yet fictional) musical career with an impressive oeuvre consisting of more than

150 albums. Each album has a hand-painted cover, protecting a painstakingly crafted record handmade out of cardboard.

THE AMATEUR DETOX FOR PROFES-SIONALS

The ability to shrug off your "baggage of experience" will undoubtedly make you a better creative. Yes, that may sound counterintuitive, but letting go of everything you know is a way of becoming better at something you're already good at. But, if you dare to approach your work from a "less informed" perspective you might just learn something... new.

The big question is... how the hell do you do that? You detox. Everyone's doing it. Everybody is not doing something in the quest for a better, seemingly purer version of themselves. But this is a detox with a difference. For starters, you can eat whatever you want, and you never know, it might just change your life. Anything is possible when you break the rules.

A detox in its simplest form is depriving oneself of something to remove toxins, create balance, break habits, and create room for self-reflection. If you believe everything you read, it will make you thinner, smarter, healthier, happier, greener, better looking, fitter, and more enlightened. Good luck with that. But what would happen if you were to apply this theory of deprivation to your work and creative processes?

This detox aims to help professional creatives shed their baggage of experience, which you will probably discover you've become quite attached to in your professional capacity. It's time to cast off everything you know and attempt to tackle your work from a "less informed" perspective.

Amateur architecture is everywhere. The creative renaissance in children's tree house design is NOW. Most of these structures would probably not pass a building

inspection and there are quite possibly lawsuits waiting
to happen, but that's part of their charm. B.Y.O. hardhat.

STEP ONE:

Break the habit. Your first step is to identify all of the things that make your work "easy" and get rid of them – only temporarily – there's no need to go throwing expensive gadgets out your window. Everything you use to speed up your creative process is taking a well-earned break.

STEP TWO:

Go analogue. Technology makes life easier, and in a lot of professional fields, it turns people into complacent, one-trick ponies. So close Photoshop, Illustrator, and PowerPoint. Switch the digital camera for an analogue one. Grab your pens and paper, paints and brushes. Want to copy-paste something? You'll need glue and scissors. Auto-pilot is no longer an option. Now you have to be more involved in the creative process. If you have to work harder and put in more effort you'll find that you think twice about whether or not this idea is the best you've got.

STEP THREE:

Borrow it. If you're dying without all of your trusty technology, try using programs and equipment that you've never used before.

STEP FOUR:

Know less. Try applying your knowledge and skills to something else. For example, apply standard design principles to gardening, fishing, washing machine repairs, or football coaching.

STEP FIVE:

Make it up. Try doing something new. But instead of diving straight into a YouTube tutorial, use the skills and knowledge you do have to come up with your solution.

STEP SIX:

Commit to being an amateur and learn something new. Learn carpentry, it might make you a more insightful art director. Learn to knit, it might enrich your skills as a writer. Make time for curiosity. Learn, make, and break – it's the creative equivalent of a multivitamin.

When I'm in a rush, I'll take the car. It gets me from A to B as quickly as possible. When I've got time, I'll take the bicycle. It lets me look around and enjoy the view. When I've got no rush, I'll walk. I've always got an umbrella handy in case it rains. When I'm completely and utterly bored, I'll take the wheels off my car, the seat off my bicycle, and the handle off my umbrella and fuse them together. It doesn't get me from A to B, it doesn't let me look around, it doesn't keep me dry in the rain, but it does keep me curious. How can three handy objects turn into something so completely and utterly useless? Useless until I find a use that is…

NOBODY WAS BORN A MASTER; AMATEURS BECOME EXPERTS

BECAUSE THEY DID NOT GIVE UP ON LEARNING.

YOU ARE GOING AS FAR AS YOU CAN
IF YOU'LL LEARN AND APPLY!

ISRAELMORE AYIVOR

RE-
MEMBER
IT

WRONG

It's one thing to remember a good idea, but it's another to
misremember a good idea and accidentally make it great.
We often misremember memories as a way of forgetting
the worst parts and idealizing the most important bits.
Ideas work the same way. Some choose to never write ideas
down, believing that they will only survive if they're good
enough to remember. But sometimes our memory has
a way of forgetting, despite us paying close attention.
For example, the Ski-Doo was supposed to be the Ski-Dog
before someone misremembered the name at the time of
registration. Or when Francis Ford Coppola was adapting
The Godfather, he famously wrote the scene where a
horse's head is discovered in a bed. The author, Mario
Puzo, explained that Coppola had actually got it wrong.
In the book, the horse was in fact found in the bedroom,
completely unmutilated, but Puzo loved Coppola's mistake.
But maybe this story isn't exactly how it happened.
Maybe it's being remembered wrong in and of itself.

MAKE TOYS,

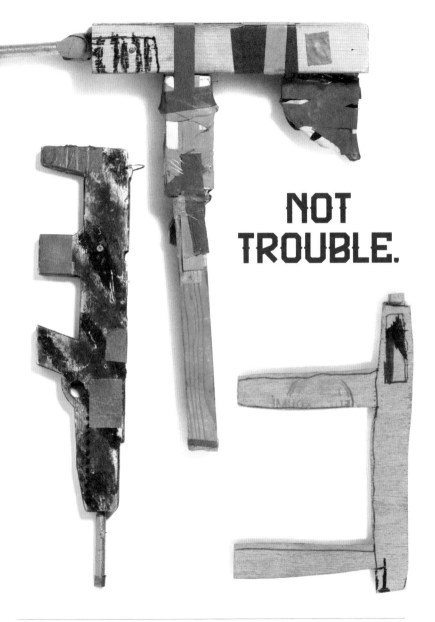

NOT
TROUBLE.

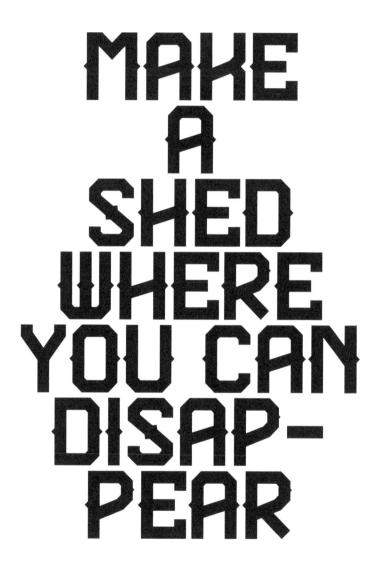

Your father didn't.
Her mother didn't either.
Oranges.
They don't rhyme with anything.
Timing is everything.
Good for you for trying.
A little quieter, please.
Now we can't hear you.
LMNOP sounds like one word when you say it too fast.
Try saying it in Spanish.
Don't learn the language first.
Cheating is useless.
Stealing is where the money is.
What was the name of that actor again?
Page 1.
Chapter 1.
How would you like your ideas: still or sparkling?

THIS PAGE

Toilets and bicycles are a very Duchamp-esque pairing. Maybe what we're looking at is a work in progress. Maybe it's finished. Maybe it's not art. Maybe it's designed for a room with two toilets (and no door, as weird as that may seem).

THE
AMATEUR
AUTHOR

I practice what I preach. Case in point: these two wooden
sculptures. If you can even call them that. I made them
when I was 12. I hesitate to use the word "designed."
First, we have a polished wooden ball. Perfectly round.
Perfectly useless. Second, we have the main course. A very
stylized duck. But that's not all. The duck is on a base.
A platform. A pedestal, if you will. And unlike the boring
ball that doesn't bounce, I was extraordinarily proud of this
duck. I signed it. I attributed this creation to myself with
purpose. The fact I put a duck on the base with my own
name is something very important because of how very
amateur it is. I was so happy with it, I put my name on it.
It's a weird thing. I tell you this not to brag, as if it's even
possible with these two artifacts. Consider this my apology
for a totally amateur work. An author's apology for the
most embarrassing thing I can show. I showed you mine,
now you show me yours.

"AN AUTHOR'S APOLOGY
FOR THE MOST EMBARRASSING THING
I CAN SHOW."

Page 8-9: Courtesy Dave Bell
Page 12: Courtesy Erik Kessels
Page 16-17: © Duc Nhan Nguyen, by SIAE 2022
Page 18-21: Photographs from Erik Kessels, *in almost every picture*, no. 7,
in collaboration with Joep Eijkens
Page 22-23: André Thijssen, *Amsterdam Neths (irregular bricks)*, 2004
© André Thijssen, by SIAE 2022
Page 24-25: Courtesy Krista Rozema
Page 30-31: © Daniel Eatock, *Fruit Sticker Bowl*, 2007, fruit stickers, ceramic bowl
Page 36-37: Courtesy Krista Rozema
Page 40-41: Courtesy Sam Barksy
Page 44-45: Photographs from Erik Kessels, *in almost every picture*, no. 15,
courtesy Sándor Kardos - Horus Archives, Budapest
Page 46-47: Helmut Smits, *Rainbow*, 2010, acrylic paint.
Photos by Lotte Stekelenburg
Page 56-58: Courtesy Bart Eysink Smeets
Page 68: Courtesy Ralph Smith
Page 72-73: Martí Guixé, *Tourist Tattoo*, 1997, photo © Inga Knölke
Page 74-75: Helmut Smits, *Nascar*, 2004, shopping bags, garbage bags,
plastic foil, tape, air
Page 76-77: Courtesy Dalton Ghetti, photo © Sloan Howard
Page 78-79: Courtesy Jens Sundheim
Page 80: Courtesy The Human Printer
Page 84-85: Courtesy Erik Kessels
Page 86-87: Thijs Verbeek, *Portrait of Lucifer - Self-initiated*, 2004-2005.
Photos by Arjan Benning
Page 88-89: Courtesy Bart Eysink Smeets
Page 90: André Thijssen, *Amsterdam Neths (dripper)*, 2000
© André Thijssen, by SIAE 2022
Page 93: Photograph from "Fascinatie" by Erik Kessels in "Adformatie".
Courtesy David de la Cruz
Page 94-95, 97: Courtesy Erik Kessels
Page 100-103: Courtesy Rop van Mierlo, *Wild Animals*, 2010
Page 106-107: © Daniele Pario Perra, by SIAE 2022
Page 109: Courtesy Thomas Mailaender
Page 110-111: Courtesy Paul Bogaers
Page 113: Courtesy Erik Kessels
Page 116-117: Courtesy Bas Kosters, photo by Marc Deurloo
Page 120-121: Courtesy Bart Eysink Smeets

Page 122-123: Courtesy Joachim Schmid
Page 124: Courtesy Erik Kessels
Page 128-129: Courtesy Thomas Mailaender
Page 130: Photograph from Erik Kessels, *in almost every picture*, no. 11, courtesy Fred & Valerie
Page 132-133: Courtesy Mingering Mike, from the workshop "Amateurism" by Erik Kessels at the Academie voor Bouwkunst Amsterdam 2008, lecture by Dori Hadar and Mingering Mike
Page 136-137: Courtesy Erik Kessels
Page 140-141: Courtesy "Amateurism" workshop by Erik Kessels, at the Academie voor Bouwkunst Amsterdam. Photo Thomas Lenden
Page 146-147: Courtesy Erik Kessels
Page 152-153: Courtesy "Amateurism" workshop by Erik Kessels, at the Academie voor Bouwkunst Amsterdam. Photo Thomas Lenden
Page 155: Courtesy Erik Kessels

Erik Kessels
Complete Amateur

Book design
Erik Kessels

English text editing: Gianni Baha

First edition July 2022

Printed in Italy by
Arti Grafiche Castello, Viadana (MN)

Maurizio Corraini s.r.l.
Via Ippolito Nievo, 7/A
46100 Mantova
Tel. 0039 0376 322753
Fax 0039 0376 365566
e-mail: info@corraini.com
www.corraini.com

START THIS BOOK

START IT WHEREVER YOU LIKE. FRONT TO
BACK. BACK TO FRONT. EITHER WAY, EVERY
DOUBLE PAGE HAS QUOTES, SHORT READS,
VISUAL EXAMPLES AND MOTIVATIONS, ALL
DESIGNED TO WORK OUT YOUR AMATEUR
MUSCLE. NO STRUCTURE. NO ORDER.